japanese detail: architecture

japanese detail: architecture

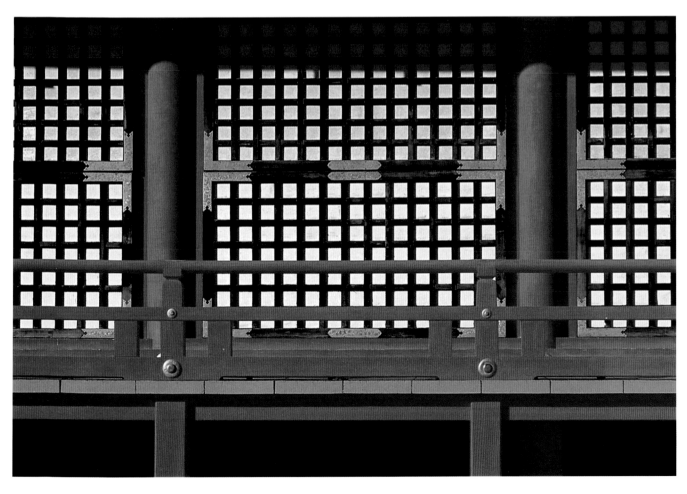

sadao hibi

CHRONICLE BOOKS
SAN FRANCISCO

First published in the United States
in 1989 by Chronicle Books LLC.

Copyright © 1987 by Sadao Hibi.

First published in Japan by
Graphic-sha Publishing Co., Ltd.

Library of Congress Cataloging-in-
Publication Data available.

ISBN 0-8118-3675-4

Manufactured in China.

Cover design by Pamela Geismar

Distributed in Canada by
Raincoast Books
9050 Shaughnessy Street
Vancouver, British Columbia V6P 6E5

10   9   8   7   6   5

Chronicle Books LLC
85 Second Street
San Francisco, California 94105

www.chroniclebooks.com

CONTENTS

Nostalgia for Color and Form in Japanese Architecture

When faced with securing life's basic necessities of food, clothing, and shelter, the Japanese have traditionally focused on shelter only after their food and clothing needs have been satisfied. Today, Japan enjoys unparalleled material abundance, which has triggered an age of unbridled consumption. But this material well-being has also elicited another response: people have begun to seek shelters that provide tranquility.

Since the early 1980s, tranquility and comfort, concepts that echo man's inner needs, have been replacing such common concerns as progress and efficiency. This change in values from the material to the spiritual, which is evident throughout Japan, demonstrates a weariness with placing progress ahead of all else. During the country's period of rapid economic expansion, its citizens rarely took an opportunity to catch their breath; now they seek quietude and free time for their own inner growth. People who only thought of pushing forward are now reviewing their actions in the search for flexible, meaningful lives.

Such reflection is readily apparent in the so-called retrospection boom, a nostalgia for the old ways that does not stop with the Taisho and Meiji eras, but goes back centuries to the Edo period. Then, people maintained an intimate relationship with material things, an association that gave their lives meaning. Only after the Second World War did materialism evolve into something that seemed greater than life itself.

A serious look at traditional homes is one result of the new respect for the past. Historically, the concepts governing Japanese architecture fully considered the natural elements of the land. The country's four distinct seasons and abundant rainfall were responsible for her scenic beauty — her "purple hills and crystal streams." The dampness, warmth, and temperate climate endowed the archipelago with magnificent forests; the logs cut from these woods in turn became the basic material in the development of the architecture. Thus, the culture of Japan became the "culture of wood."

In a country so richly blessed by nature, Japanese architects strove to work in harmony with, not confront, the environment. Unlike their European counterparts, whose extraordinary stone structures often evoked images of manmade fortresses designed to ward off nature's severity, the Japanese built homes of clay and wood, materials that both illustrated humanity's need for what is natural and acknowledged the importance of grass and trees in people's lives.

The hedge or fence that surrounds the traditional Japanese house, for example, is not intended to guard against the outside world. Its purpose is just the contrary. Rather than acting as a protective wall, the design conveys a feeling of openness to those looking on. As tree leaves rustle in the wind and flickering lights spill out, one is drawn to the house with a sense of intimacy, of kinship.

Now consider the shoji, the sliding door. The paper pasted over the door's wooden framework gives off a soft, gentle feeling in contrast to the world outside. The light filtering through the white paper and casting shadows upon the tatami mat relates how nature is faring. As the sun disappears beyond the horizon in the late afternoon, the evening lamplight projects a silhouette of those working or sitting around the fireside onto the shoji. In summer, the whiteness of the paper provides a pleasurable counterpoint to the vivid green of nature. In winter, there is no better way to look upon a garden cloaked in white than to sip heated sake and nibble on foods while peering through a snow-viewing shoji. Through this wood-and-paper partition, the tenant, though caught up in the routine of daily living, is able to appreciate the artistic effects of the changing seasons.

As has been explained, the classic architecture of Japan, sired and nurtured by the country's four distinct seasons, was based on a harmonious relationship with nature. The traditional concept of beauty, however, was split into two opposing schools of color and form.

On the one hand, beige and gray were highly prized colors, as they underscored the taste for the natural — the elegant simplicity of *sabi* and the quietness and frugality of *wabi*. Maximum use was made of the colors of clay, trees, straw, and cogongrass to produce a refined, subdued beauty that was *shibui*; at the same time, all garish hues were rejected.

The deeper one delves into history, the clearer one becomes on how the Japanese came to appreciate this form of beauty. Admiration for the spare and frugal may be said to have been advocated by Takeno Jo-o and then brought to a culmination by Senno Rikyu, who was responsible for the Soan tea ceremony room. A verse from the *Shin Kokin Wakashu* vividly summarizes the simplicity of the setting:

> From this teahouse, not a flower or tinted leaf in sight: how glorious the autumn twilight above the water.
>
> Fujiwara-no-teika

Opposing the school of "colorless aesthetics" was a group that maintained a strong infatuation with bright, resplendent colors. If the proponents of simplicity represented a world of shadows in the moonlight, the latter school symbolized the world of light with the sun as its centerpiece. Some representative architectural works of the ornamental style are Toyotomi Hideyoshi's Golden Tea Ceremonial Hall and the Tokugawa family's Nikko Toshogu Shrine.

In the past, most Japanese houses adopted plain, natural colors. Aside from feudal lords and wealthy merchants, the citizenry lived humbly from day to day in spaces showing only somber color tones. It is possible to see how the masses adapted to their homes during the lighted hours of the day and the darkness of the night by inspecting old structures in many parts of the country.

A good place to visit is the Nihon Minka-en Park at Kawasaki, an outdoor museum in Kanagawa Prefecture. Traditional homes of common people, only a few of which still stand in the country today, were disassembled, brought to the park, and carefully reconstructed. Readily evident is the magnificent *gassho* architecture of Hida, the Shirakawa region, and Etchu Gokayama. There is the Kujukurihama home of the boss of the net-laying fishermen, where one can almost hear the heavy footsteps of the men of the sea. Homes of wealthy merchants of Nara and Ina. A kabuki stage from Funakoshi. Altogether there are over twenty structures, including a mill with a waterwheel, a grain warehouse, and a mortuary temple, spread throughout this quiet, spacious landscape.

My visit to the park on an early autumn day was punctuated by a light drizzle. The structures were dimly lit and a musky smell of dirt filled the air. As I toured the buildings, two things weighed heavily on my mind: a feeling of nostalgia and a sense of darkness that pervaded each house.

At that moment, I felt as if I had unraveled the mystery as to why people in olden times used so much color in festivals and places of worship. To those whose living spaces were always marked with darkness, lustrous colors represented something fresh and vivid, to be used only in festivals or on special occasions. Combinations of colors that sent the mind reeling and bright lights that glowed with the brilliance of gold dazzled people unfamiliar with such richness in their daily lives. It then struck me that even the crimson red *torii* shrine archway should not be dismissed as simply vulgar.

By unashamedly seeking bright colors, these Japanese found a venue of escape from their day to day existence. Flamboyant hues provided them with momentary release, thereby maintaining an admirable sense of balance between the everyday and the special.

Ayako Jindai

1 . *Shoin* (reading alcove) Katsurarikyu (Imperial Villa) (Kyoto)

2. Private residence, Ōhara (Kyoto)

3 . Pillars of Kondō Hall, Tōshōdaiji Temple (Nara)

4 . *Azekura* (type of storehouse) at Tōshōdaiji Temple (Nara)

5 . The *torii* at Fushimi Inari (Kyoto)

6 . *Tenshukaku* (keep) at Hikonejō Castle (Shiga)

ROOFS
屋根

The forms of roofs vary with the topography and the society for which they were built. By gazing from a tall building at rows of houses, one can imagine from the roofs alone the lives of each of the inhabitants.

7. Thirteen-storied pagoda, Danzan Shrine (Nara)

8. Tiled roof (Nara)

9. *Gyōki-buki* roof, Gankōji Temple (Nara)

10. Tiled roof, Konponchūdō Hall, Enryakuji Temple (Shiga)

11. Thatched roof and *katsuogi* (at top), Karasu Shrine (Ise, Mie)

12. Five-storied pagoda, Meiōin (Hiroshima)

13. Shingled roof, Mirokudō Hall, Murouji Temple (Kyoto)

14. Straw-thatched roof of a private residence, Nose (Osaka)

15. Private residence with a *kabuto-zukuri* (helmet-shaped) roof, Nishi Tama (Tokyo)

16. Straw-thatched roof and *munekazari* (crest decoration) of a private residence, Shūzan (Wakasa, Fukui)

17. *Suzumeodori* (cresting named for its fancied resemblance to a sparrow dancing) of the Horiuchi residence (Shiojiri, Nagano)

18. Plaster roof of a private residence (Chōsi, Chiba)

19. Weighted roof (Tsumago, Nagano)

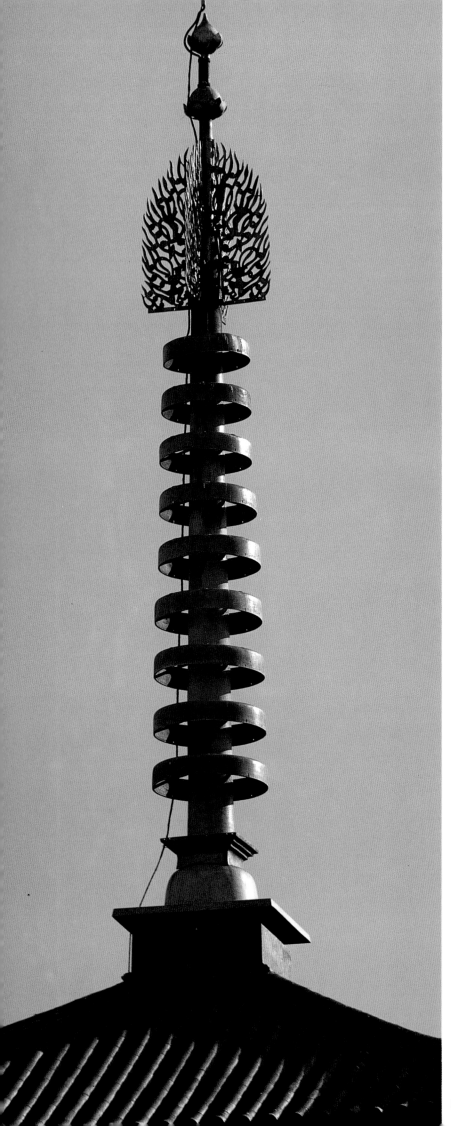

21. *Hōkeikazari* (crest resembling a hair ornament) and tiled roof, Hōryūji Temple (Nara)

22. *Rokumonsen* crest and pair of *shachihoko*, Main Hall, Chokokuji Temple (Nagano)

20. *Sōrin* of the Eastern Tower, Yakushiji Temple (Nara)

23. A chrysanthemum crest, Shugankuinrikyu (Imperial Villa), Kyusuitei (Kyoto)

24. A roof decoration depicting the legendary Chinese phoenix, Shugankuinrikyu Chitose bridge

25. *Shachihoko* atop of the *tenshukaku* of Kaminoyamajō Castle (Yamagata)

26. *Tomoe* (swirl designs), Jōnangū Shrine (Kyoto)

23

27. *Oni-gawara* (ogre gargoyle), Main Hall, Jindōji Temple (Kyoto) 28. *Oni-gawara*, Hōryūji Temple (Nara)

29. *Mon-gawara* (circular tiles engraved with family crests), Himejijō Castle (Hyōgo)

KAERUMATA
蟇股

The *kaerumata*, a carving enshrined on a beam, takes its name (literally, ''frog's crotch'') from its shape. The *kaerumata* was originally used to support the weight of the roof, but it is now preserved as an ornament.

30. *Tokyō* (eaves support), Kondō Hall, Taime-dera Temple (Nara)

31. *Kaerumata* (interbeam support) with a peony carving on a gate of Jōshōji Temple (Nagano)

32. *Kaerumata*, Mandala Hall, Taima-dera Temple (Nara)

33. *Kaerumata*, Jōdōji Temple (Hiroshima)

34. *Kaerumata*, Kitanotenmangū Shrine (Osaka)

35. *Tennyo* (celestial nymph) carving, Shoshido Hall, Myōjōji Temple (Ishikawa)

36. *Kaerumata* with a carving of a crane flying over clouds, Chōgosonji Temple (Nara)

37. *Tennyo* (celestial nymph) carving, Soshidō Hall, Myōjōji Temple

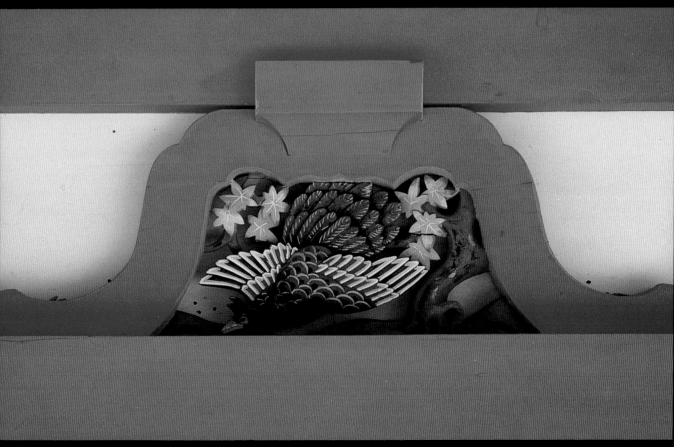

38. *Kaerumata* with a peacock carving, Chōgosonji Temple

39. *Kaerumata* and carvings, Nijōjō Castle (Kyoto)

40. Carving of tigers in a bamboo thicket on the gate at Sengen Shrine (Shizuoka)

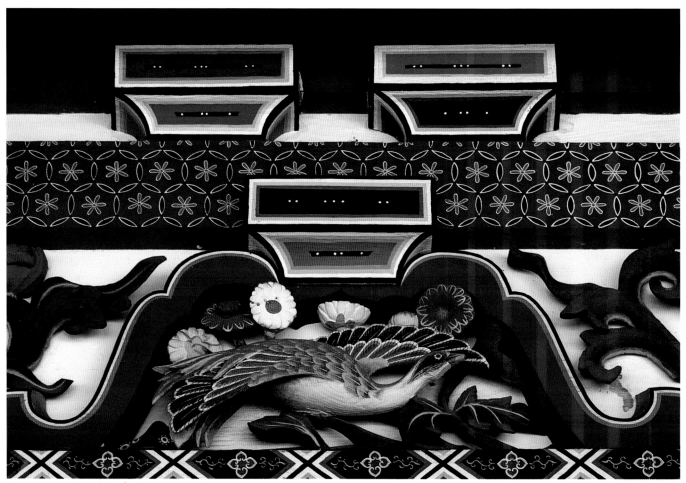

41. Carving of a bird and flowers, Ōsaki Hachiman Shrine (Sendai, Miyagi)

42. Carving of a waterfowl and irises on the gate at Sengen Shrine

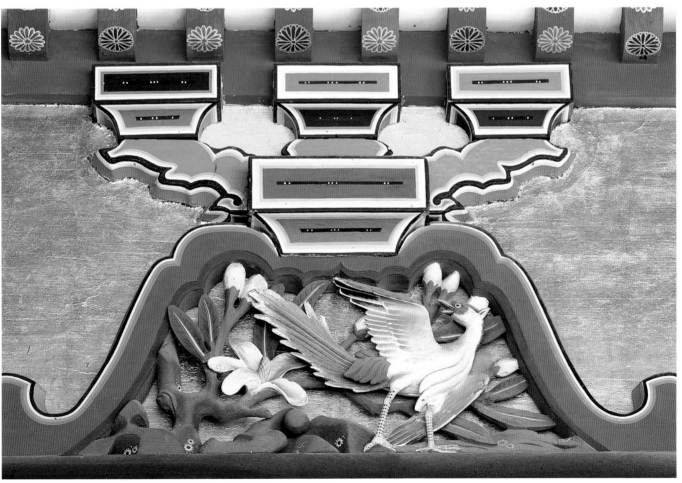

43. Carving of a bird and flowers, Ōsaki Hachiman Shrine

44. *Kaerumata* with a peony carving, Isonokami Shrine (Nara)

45. A crane carving, Myoenji Hondo, Tango

WALLS

壁

The Japanese wall is like a natural element, always transformed by its surroundings but always in harmony with them. Both the white walls of a castle and of a merchant's home are designed to impart a sense of peace.

A red-walled warehouse, Kurashiki, Okayama

47. White-walled storehouse (Kurashiki)

48. *Namako kabe* (wall) (Kurashiki)

49. *Namako kabe* of the Seisonkaku (Ishikawa)

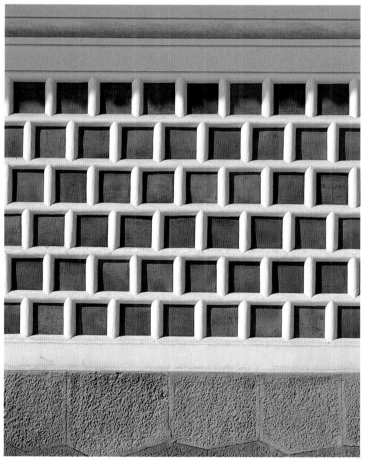

50. *Namako kabe* of a merchant's house (Iga Ueno, Mie)

51. Gun embrasures in a white wall, Himejijō Castle (Hyōgo)

52. Board fence of private residence (Takayama, Gifu)

53. Board fence of the Honma residence (Yamagata)

54. *Benigara kabe* (rust-colored wall), Sentō Imperial Palace (Kyoto)

55. Wall of a tea-ceremony room, Yasukuni Shrine (Tokyo)

LATTICEWORK

格子

Stylish latticework houses can still be found in neighborhoods that were once the pleasure quarters. Lattice-work windows and walls allowed the seductive sounds of laughter and *shamisen* music to drift into the streets, enticing passers-by.

57. *Shitomi-do* (hanging latticed door), Daihōonji Temple (Kyoto)

58. *Renji mado* (latticed window), Tōshōdaiji (Nara)

59. *Renji mado*, Usa Hachimangū Shrine (Ōita)

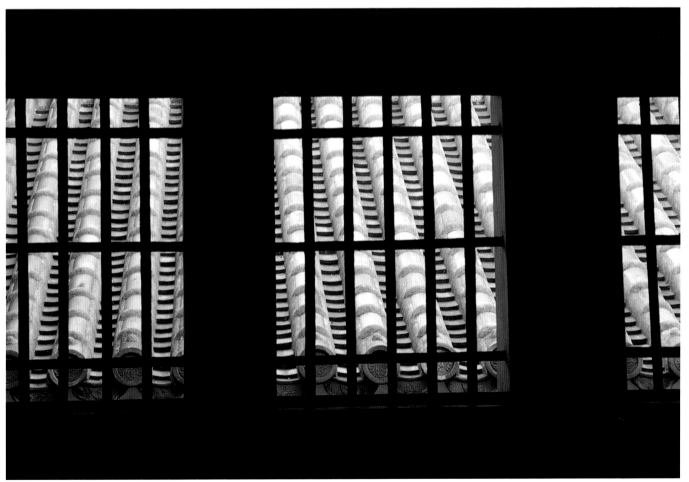

60. Iron-barred windows, Himejijō Castle (Hyōgo)

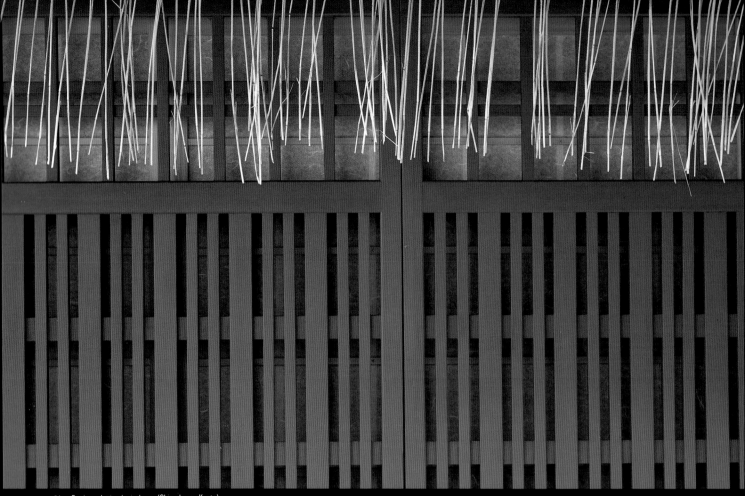

61. *Benigara* latticed windows (Shimabara, Kyoto)

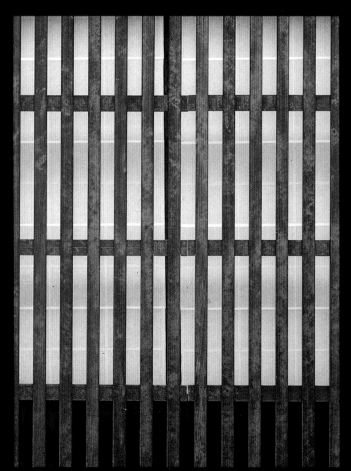

62. Latticed window of a merchant's house (Narai, Kiso, Nagano)

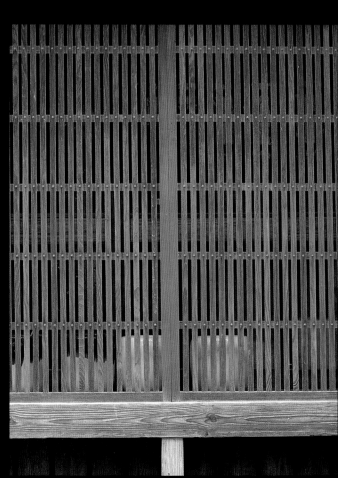

63. Latticed window of a private residence (Miyajima, Hiroshima)

64. Latticed window of a private residence (Takayama, Gifu)

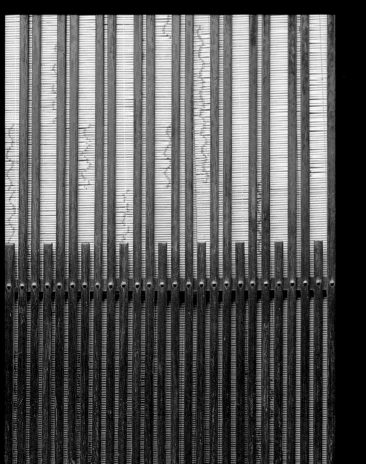

65. Latticed window of a private residence (Takayama)

66. Latticed window of a private residence (Gion, Kyoto)

67. *Ranma* (above) and latticed door, Hōryūji Temple (Nara)

68. *Ranma* and latticed door, Sangatsudō Hall, Tōdaiji Temple (Nara)

WINDOWS

窓

The window is the source of a house's fresh air and light, a space that links man to the outside world. It is through the windows of a house that the inhabitants witness the changes of the seasons, the passage of time.

69. Window of a private residence (Imai, Nara)

70. Windows of the Kōgitei (Matsushiro, Nagano)

71. Latticework and *shōji* (sliding paper door) (Kurashiki, Okayama)

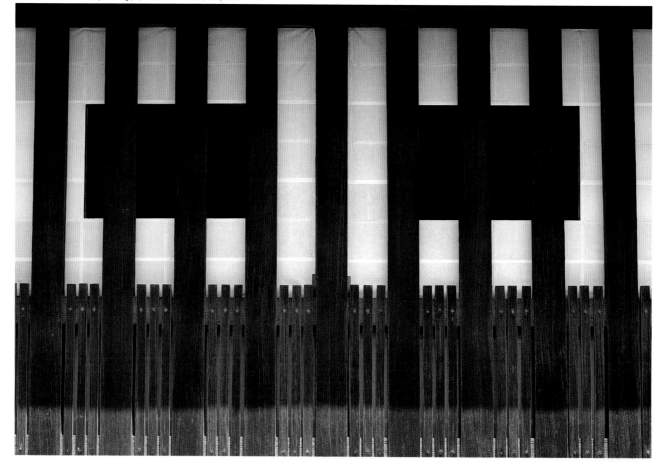

72. Window *shōji* of a private residence (Mibu, Kyoto)

73. Lattice window of a private residence (Nose, Osaka)

74. *Demado* (bay window) (Yorikimon, Osaka)

75. *Demado* of a samurai's residence (Takahashi, Okayama)

76. *Demado* of a samurai's residence (Kanazwa, Ishikawa)

77. Windows on a merchant's house built in the *kura-zukuri* (fireproof warehouse) style (Kawagoe, Saitama)

78. Windows on a merchant's house built in the *kura-zukuri* style (Kawagoe)

79. *Dozō mado* (window of an erthern house or storehouse) (Kyoto)

80. *Dozō mado* (Tango, Kyoto)

81. Storehouse window (Kurashiki, Okayama)

82. Storehouse window (Kurashiki)

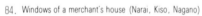

83. Windows of a private residence (Shirakawa, Gifu)

84. Windows of a merchant's house (Narai, Kiso, Nagano)

85. *Tenshukaku,* Himejijō Castle (Hyōgo)

86. The lattice window of a merchant's house, Takayama

87. Round window, Okunoin, Taima-dera Temple (Nara)

88. Round window of a tea ceremony room, Daichiji Temple (Shiga)

89. Round window, Fundain, Tōfukuji Temple (Kyoto)

90. Round latticework window, Main Hall, Hōfukuji Temple (Okayama)

91. Round window in a sanctuary, Chikudensö (Ôita)

92. Round window of a tea ceremony room, Sentô Imperial Palace (Kyoto)

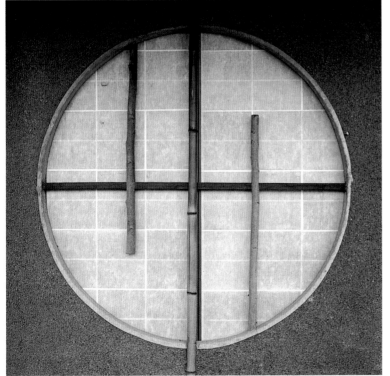

93. Round window Chikudensö

94. Window in the waiting room, Meimeian (Matsue, Shimane)

95. *Katō mado* (window of Zen architecture), Ginkakuji (Kyoto)

96. *Katō mado*, Main Hall, Fudōin (Hiroshima)

97. *Katō mado*, abbot's chamber, Myōshinji Temple (Kyoto)

98. *Katō mado*, Seihakuji Temple (Yamanashi)

GATES
門

From the gate—the "face" of the house—one can often judge the character and tastes of the head of the house. In early times, the gate represented the ultimate in design and has come to be considered the highest expression of architecture.

99. Main gate (detail) of Himejijō Castle (Hyōgo)

100. Hishi-no-mon Gate, Himejijō Castle (Hyōgo)

101. Ru-no-mon Gate, Himejijō Castle

102. *Kugurimon* (wicket gate), Himejijō Castle

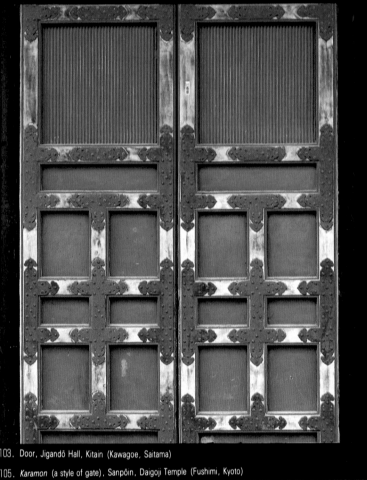

103. Door, Jigandō Hall, Kitain (Kawagoe, Saitama)

104. Door, Main Hall, Meiōin (Hiroshima)

105. *Karamon* (a style of gate), Sanpōin, Daigoji Temple (Fushimi, Kyoto)

106. *Kabutomon* (gate resembling a samurai's helmet), Konnichian, Urasenke (Kyoto)

107. *Nakakuguri* (gate at a tea-ceremony garden), Fushin'an, Omotesenke (Kyoto)

108. *Chūmon* ("middle gate"), Katsura Imperial Villa (Kyoto)

109. *Rojimon* (entrance gate of a tea-ceremony garden), Saiōin (Kyoto)

110. *Rojimon*, Kenden'an (Matsue, Shimane)

111. *Amigasamon* ("bamboo hat gate"), Mushakōjisenke (Kyoto)

112. Main gate, Katsura Imperial Villa (Kyoto)

113. *Orido* (folding door) of a tea ceremony house, Nagoyajō Castle (Aichi)

Orido at the entrance of a merchant's house (Kurashiki, Okayama)

115. *Karamon*, Kannondō Hall, Hōgenji Temple (Shiga)

116. Gate at Okayamajō Castle (Okayama)

117. *Karamon*, Nishihonganji Temple (Kyoto)

118. *Ōtemon* (main gate), Kōchijō Castle (Kōchi)

119. Metal handle on the door of the Imanishi residence (Nara)

120. Metal piece on the gate, Ōyamazumi Shrine (Ehime)

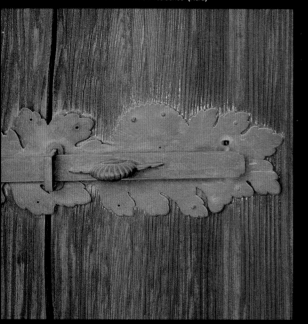

121. Metal bolt, Tōkaian, Myōshinji Temple (Kyoto)

122. Metal piece on the gate of the Honma residence (Yamagata)

123. Metal piece on the Ru-no-mon Gate, Himejijō Castle (Hyōgo)

124. Metal piece on the *ōtemon*, Ōsakajō Castle (Osaka)

The door is the protector of the home, keeping out wind, rain, and thieves. The qualities desired in a door are reliability, functionality, ease in movement, and beauty.

125. Door of the Horiuchi residence (Shiojiri, Nagano)

126. Paper sliding doors of *kazumachaya* (cafe or restaurant) (Igaueno, Mie)

127. Entrance to an inn (Narai, Kiso, Nagano)

128. Entrance to a merchant's house (Narai)

129. Entrance to the Yoshimura residence (Osaka)

130. Entrance to an inn (Magome, Kiso, Nagano)

131. Entrance to an inn (Magome)

132. Entrance to merchant's house, Hida Takayama (Gifu)

133. Lattice door of a merchant's house (Sasayama, Kyoto)

134. *Maira-dō* (door with narrowly spaced crosspieces), Tōkaian, Myōshinji Temple (Kyoto)

135. Door to a storehouse (Kurashiki, Okayama)

136. Door to a storehouse (Kurashiki)

137. Door in the gate of Hikonejō Castle (Shiga)

138. Door to the *azekura*, Tōshōdaiji Temple (Nara)

71

139. Door to the Higashi Muro (east room), Tōshōdaiji Temple (Nara)

Design of Japanese Architecture
Shinto shrine and Buddhist sanctum

① *Kotaijingu, Seiden* (main temple)

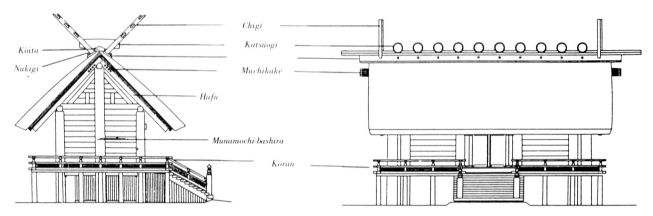

Chigi
Katsuogi
Muchikake
Hafu
Köita
Nukigi
Munamochi-bashira
Koran

② *Horuji, Kondo* (main hall of a Buddhist temple)

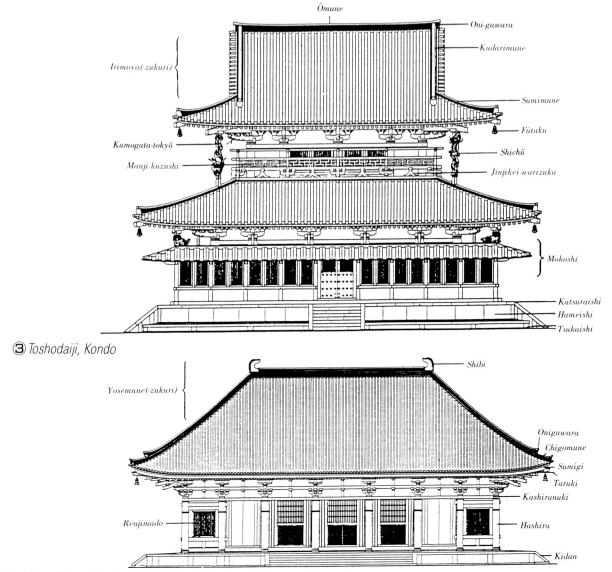

Ōmune
Oni-gawara
Kudarimune
Irimoya(-zukuri)
Sumimune
Fūtaku
Kumogata-tokyō
Shichū
Manji-kuzushi
Jinjikei-warizuka
Mokoshi
Katsuraishi
Hameishi
Tsukaishi

③ *Toshodaiji, Kondo*

Shibi
Yosemune(-zukuri)
Onigawara
Chigomune
Sumigi
Taruki
Kashiranuki
Renjimado
Hashira
Kidan

(1) from "Jingu" (Shogakukan Inc.)
(2,3) from "Nippon Kenchiku Kiso Shiryo Shusei" (Chuokoron Bijyutsu Shuppan)

Door

Karado (paneled door)

San-karado
(paneled door with ledges)

San-karado

Karado

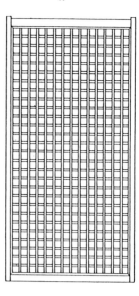 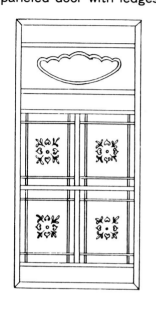 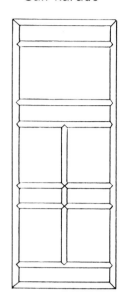 

Sliding paper door *(shōji)*

Kumiko-shōji

(fretted sliding paper door)

Butsuma-shōji

(sliding paper door)

Yukimi-shōji

(snow viewing sliding paper door)

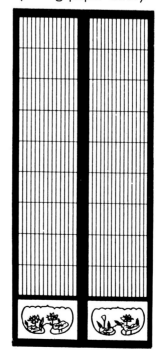 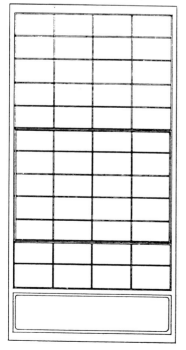

(1-7) from "Tategu Hinagata Zenshu" (Kosaku-sha, Inc.)

Alcove and Shelves

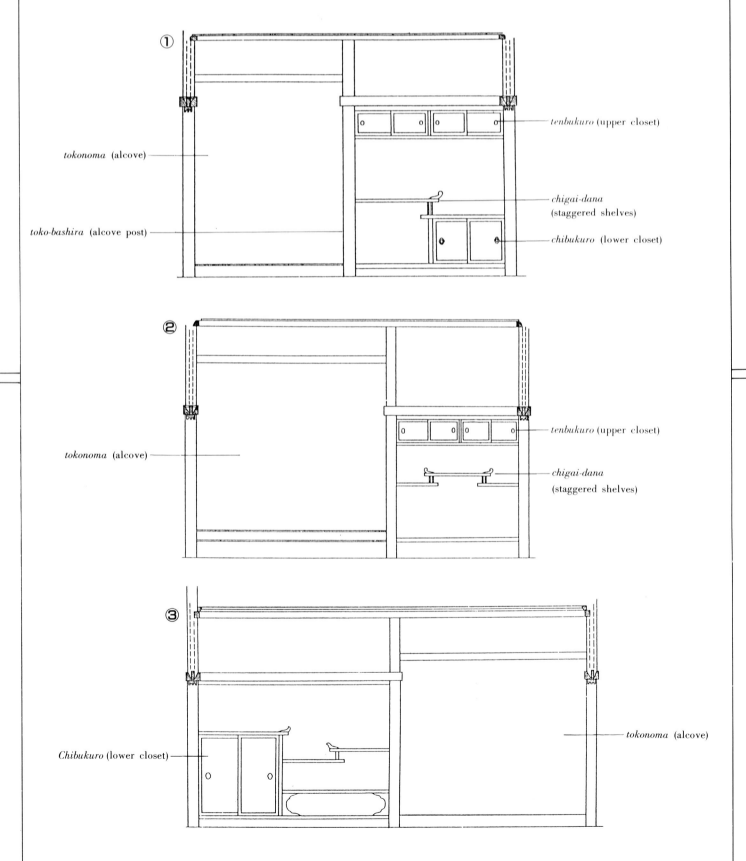

① *tenbukuro* (upper closet)

tokonoma (alcove)

chigai-dana (staggered shelves)

toko-bashira (alcove post)

chibukuro (lower closet)

② *tenbukuro* (upper closet)

tokonoma (alcove)

chigai-dana (staggered shelves)

③ *tokonoma* (alcove)

Chibukuro (lower closet)

(1-3) from "Nippon Jyutaku Kenchiku Zuan Hyakushu" (Kenchiku Shoin)

Gate and Wall

Chūmon (middle gate)

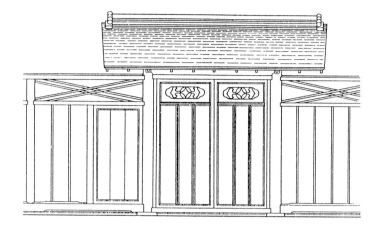

Itabei (wooden wall)

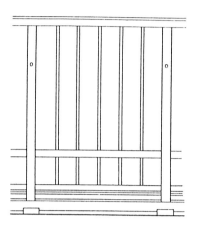

Munemon (gate with a ridge)

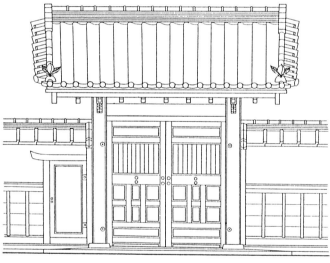

Nagashibei
(wall with horizontals of timber)

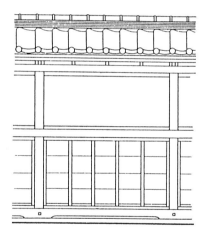

Kabukimon (roofed gate)

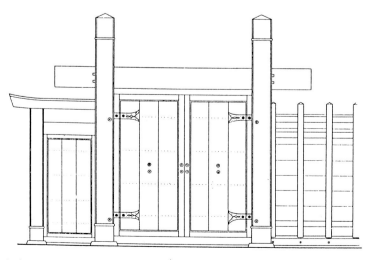

Kakusaku Itabei
(wooden wall with fence of timber)

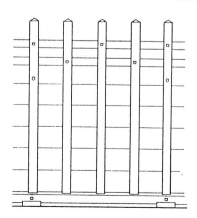

(1-6) from "Nippon Jyutaku Kenchiku Zuan Hyakushu" (Kenchiku Shoin)

SLIDING DOORS AND SLIDING PAPER DOORS
襖・障子

Both movable and removable, the sliding door reflects the flexibility and functionality of Japanese architecture. When these doors are made of paper, allowing soft light and unobtrusive privacy, that functionality is combined with delicacy.

140. *Fusuma* (sliding door) to the "first room," Nakaochaya, Shugakuin Imperial Villa (Kyoto)

141. *Fusuma* with painting of an old pine tree, Daitsūji Temple (Shiga)

142. *Fusuma* with painting of millet and quail, Jōkōji Temple (Wakasa, Fukui)

143. *Fusuma* to the "first room", Shimoochaya, Shūgakuin Imperial Villa

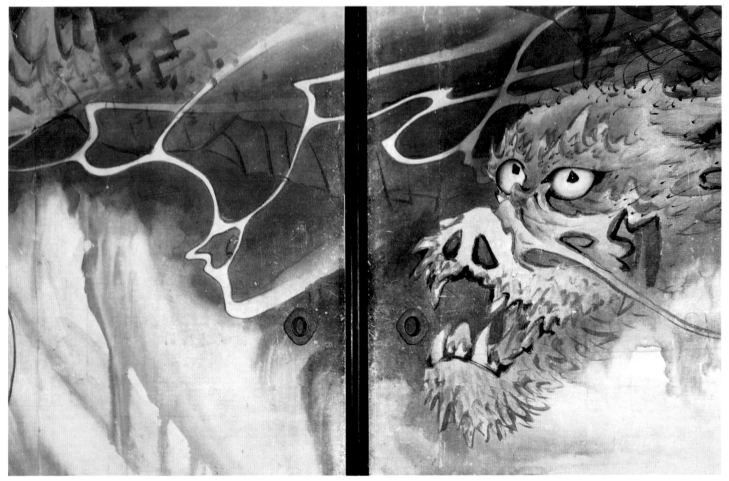

144. *Fusuma* with painting of a dragon and a tiger by Rosetsu Nagasawa, Muryōji Temple (Wakayama)

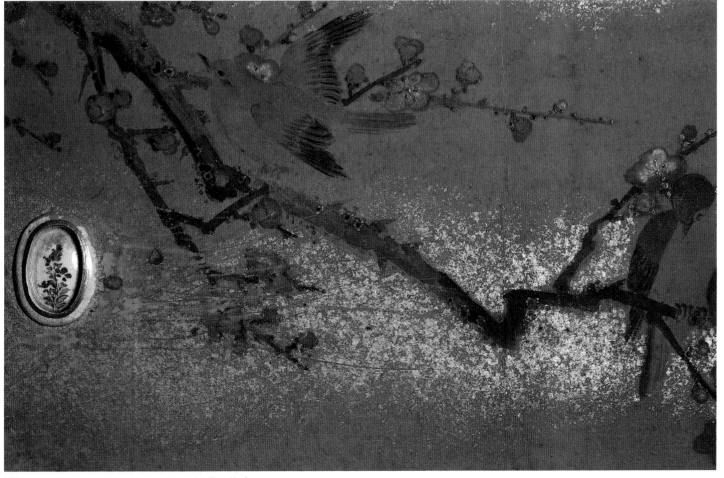

145. *Fusuma* with painting of birds and flowers, Shigetomisō (Kagoshima)

146. *Fusuma* to the "second room," Nakaochaya, Shūgakuin Imperial Villa

147. *Fusuma* with a painting of Mount Fuji, Tokujōji Temple (Kyoto)

148. Cedar door with painting of festival floats, Nakaochaya, Shūgakuin Imperial Villa

149. Cedar door with painting of rooster, Daitsūji Temple (Shiga)

150. Cedar door with *Shippō* folding fans

151. Cedar door of a guest room, Nakaochaya, Shūgakuin Imperial Villa

152. Cedar door of a guest room, Nakaochaya, Shūgakuin Imperial Villa

153. *Shōji* (sliding paper door) and *ranma* with a folding-fan shape (Osaka)

54. Snow-viewing *shōji* at the Rokumoto residence (Nara)

155. *Shōji* at the Kyōtei (Yorii, Saitama)

56. Round windows and *shōji* of the Shōiken, Katsura Imperial Villa

157. *Hikite* (hollow metal handle) in the *fusuma* at the Nakaochaya,Shūgakuin Imperial Villa

158. *Hikite* in the shape of a folding fan

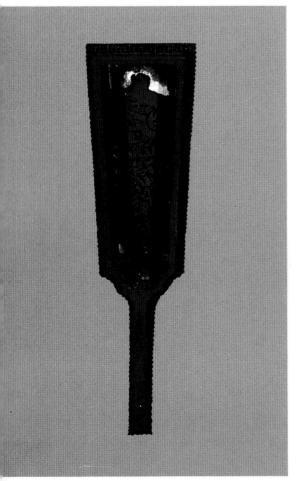

159. Hikite in the shape of Hagoita (a battledore), Shugakuinrikyu Ichinoma-Nakaochaya.

160. *Hikite* at the Naraya (Hakone, Kanagawa)

ALCOVES AND STAGGERED SHELVES
床の間・棚

The origins of the alcove and staggered shelves go back to the *shoin* architecture of the Muromachi period (1336–1573). The alcove is the place for a family's treasures—a hanging scroll, a flower arrangement.

161. *Tokonoma* (alcove) at the Oka residence

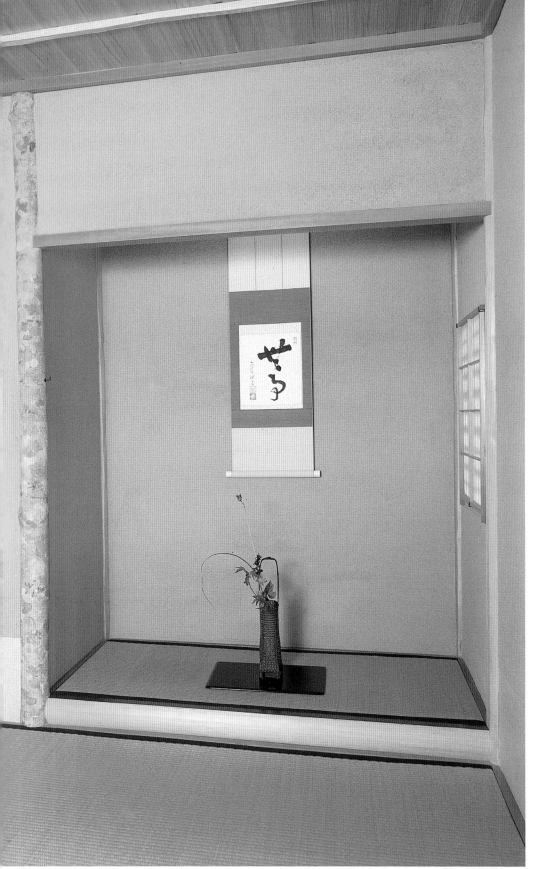

162. *Tokonama* of Kasuikan (Fukushima)

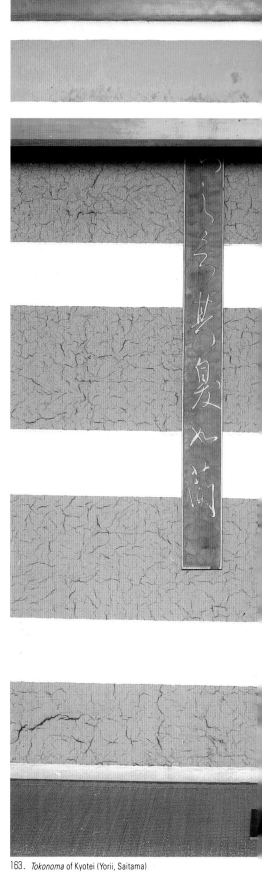

163. *Tokonoma* of Kyotei (Yorii, Saitama)

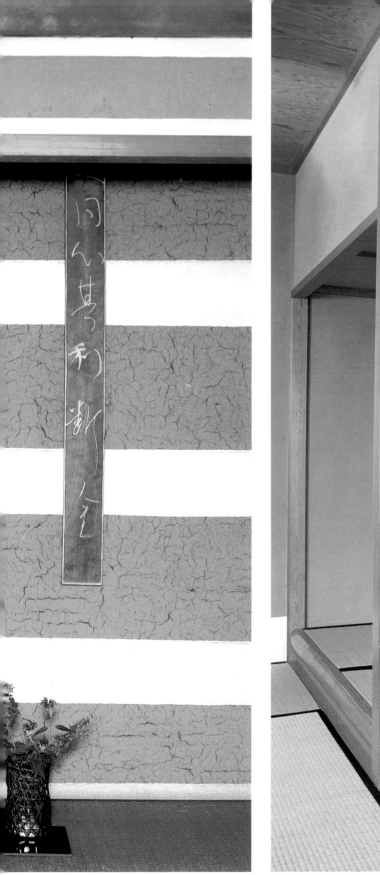

164. Tokonoma 'Horai' (a holy place named for the legendary Chinese mountain where Sennin, or a sacred hermit, lives), Atami Shizuoka.

165. Staggered shelves, Jōkōji Temple (Wakasa, Fukui)

166. Staggered shelves, the "first room," Nakaochaya, Shūgakuin Imperial Villa

167. *Ranma* with openwork of horseman crossing a river

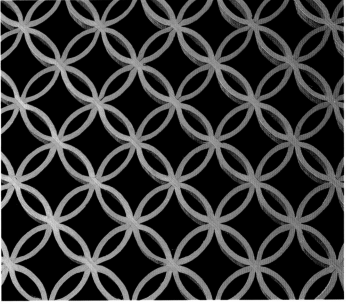

168. *Ranma* with a *Shippō-tsunagi* (overlapping ellipse) openwork, Morikawa residence (Tawaramoto, Nara)

169. *Ranma* with a *Shippō-tsunagi* openwork, Morikawa residence

170. *Ranma* with latticework, Morikawa residence

171. *Ranma* with hemp-leaf pattern, Morikawa residence

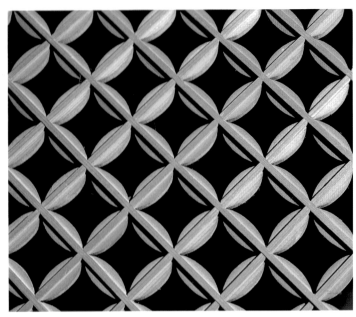

172. *Ranma* with a *Shippō-tsunagi* openwork, Morikawa residence

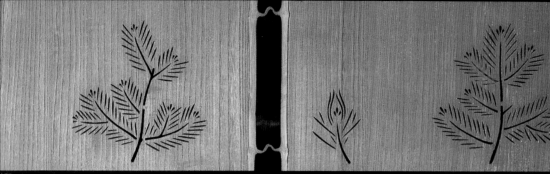

173. *Ranma* with openwork of pine trees, the Satō residence (Fujiidera, Osaka)

174. *Ranma* with openwork of plum trees, the Satō residence

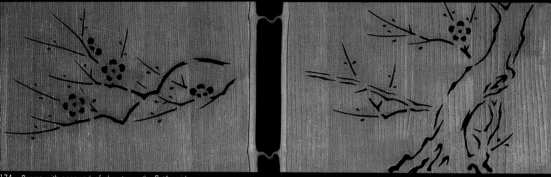

175. *Ranma* with openwork of pawlonia, Tokujōji Temple (Kyoto)

176. *Ranma* with openwork of a bird and flowers, the Satō residence

177. *Ranma* with openwork of legendary Chinese phoenix, Kasuikan (Fukushima)

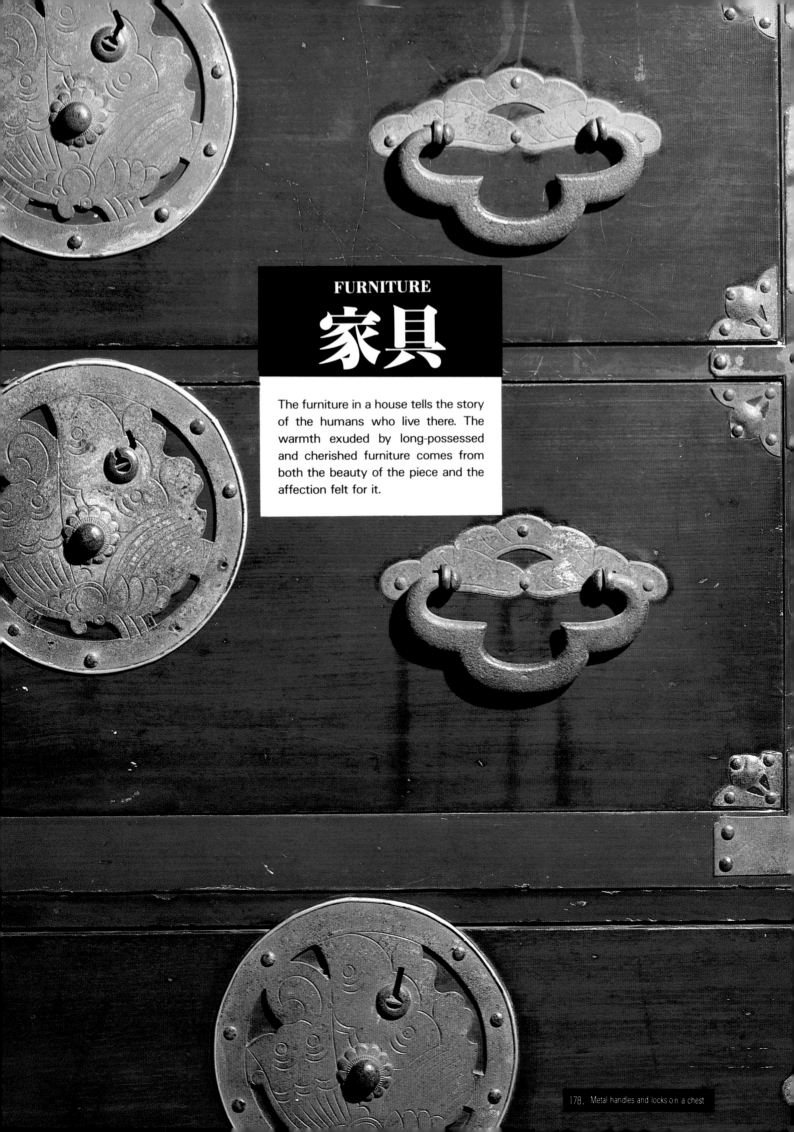

FURNITURE

家具

The furniture in a house tells the story of the humans who live there. The warmth exuded by long-possessed and cherished furniture comes from both the beauty of the piece and the affection felt for it.

178. Metal handles and locks on a chest

179. Round clock

181. Yaguradokei (turret clock).

182. Turret clock

180. Wall clock

183. *Funa-dansu*
(captain's chest)

185. Cabinet

184. *Funa-dansu*

186. *Tebunko* (stationary chest)

187. *Nagamochi*
(oblong trunk)

188. *Choba dansu* (clerical cabinet)

189. Pawlonia chest

190. Chest

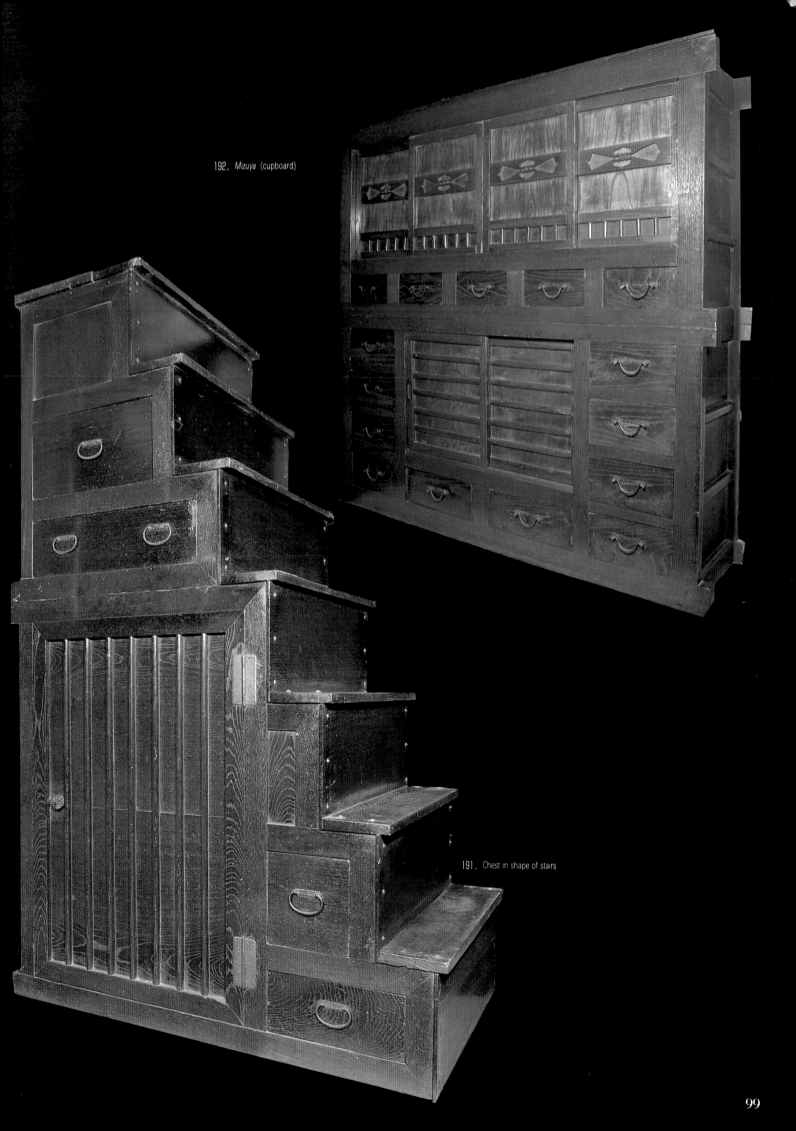

192. *Mizuya* (cupboard)

191. Chest in shape of stairs

193. Lamp

194. Lamp

195. *Andon* (oil lamp with paper shade)

196. Desk lamp

197. *Teshoku* (long-handled candlestick)

198. Lampshade

199. *Chōchin* (paper lantern)

200. *Andon*

201. Hand warmer with gold and silver lacquer design

202. Hand warmer

203. *Hako hibachi* (hibachi in the shape of a box)

204. Porcelain hibachi

205. *Hako hibachi*

206. Pawlonia hibachi

Irori (in-floor hearth) at the Kita residence (Ishikawa)

208. Rain water tank (Narai, Kiso, Nagano)

209. Water tank for fires (Takayama, Gifu)

210. Water tank for fires (Shimabara, Kyoto)

SHOP CURTAINS AND SIGNBOARDS
暖簾・看板

Designed to catch the eyes of passers-by, the shop's curtain and signboard are its lifeline. The marks of time on the signboard of a long-established enterprise are sources of pride and honor.

212. *Noren* of an *obi* (kimono sash) shop (Nishijin, Kyoto)

213. *Noren* of a liquor store (Kurashiki, Okayama)

214. *Noren* of a kimono shop (Tango, Kyoto)

215. *Noren* of a rice shop (Nara)

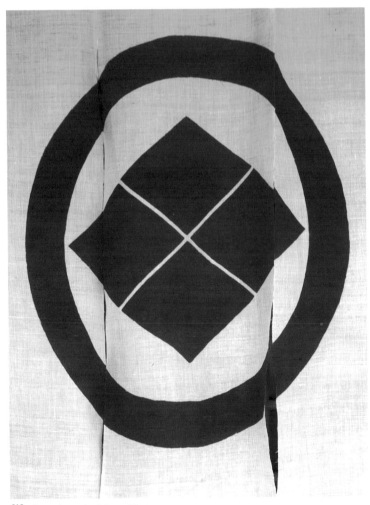

216. *Noren* of a merchant's house (Gion)

217. *Noren* of a restaurant (Shimabara, Kyoto)

218. *Noren*

219. *Noren* of a *kusakabetei* (Takayama, Gifu)

220. *Noren* of a restaurant (Shimabara, Kyoto)

221. *Noren* of a restaurant (Gion, Kyoto)

222. *Noren* with pattern of a three-leaf hollyhock, Takamatsujō Castle (Kagawa)

223. *Noren* with a camellia pattern

224. *Kaga noren* (noren of the Kaga region) (Ishikawa, Kanazawa)

225. *Kaga noren* with a pattern of a pawlonia, pine, bamboo, and plum

226. *Kaga noren* (Ishikawa, Kanazawa)

227. *Kaga noren* (Ishikawa, Kanazawa)

228. *Noren* with folding-fan pattern

229. *Noren* with paper umbrella pattern (Narai, Kiso, Nagano)

230. *Noren* depicting the sun and moon

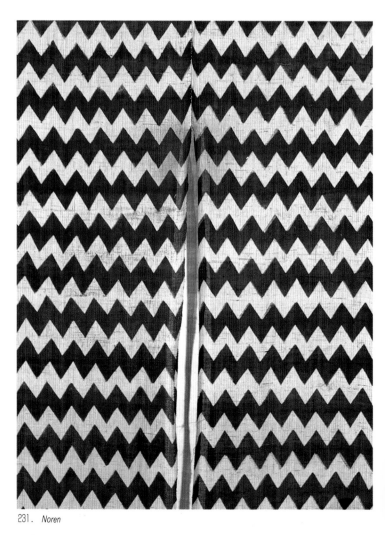

231. *Noren*

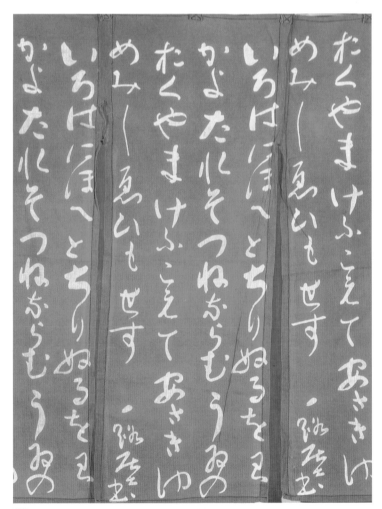

232. *Noren* showing the *iroha* (Japanese *hiragana* order)

233. *Noren* of the public bath

234. *Takenoren* (bamboo *noren*) (Kyoto)

235. *Nawa noren* (rope *noren*)

236. *Chōchin* (Kyoto)

237. *Noren* of a candy store (Kanazawa, Ishikawa)

239. *Andon* (Narai, Kiso, Nagano)

238. *Noren* of a tea store (Kyoto)

240. *Noren* of a pharmaceuticals wholesaler (Toyama)

242. Signboard of a *soba* (buckwheat noodle) shop (Takefo, Fukui)

243. A wood-curing signboard, Toyama.

244. Signboard

241. Festival *chôchin* (Iga Ueno, Mie)

245. Moneychanger's signboard

113

246. Saw sharpener's signboard

247. Signboard of a drugstore

FLAGSTONE PATHS

敷石

A flagstone path combines functionality with beauty to enhance the garden. The contrast of the wet flagstone
path and its lush surrounding greenery
is refreshing and relaxing.

249. Flagstones, Hama Imperial Villa (Tokyo)

250. Patterns of the paving stones, *hifumi-ishi* of Rinuntei, Kamiochaya Shugakuinrikyu.

251. Flagstone path, Hōjuin, Hōryūji Temple (Nara)

252. Flagstone pavement, Chikudendō (Oita)

253. A pattern of stone paving, Ochidanijinja, Tottori.

254. Stone path, Nanshūji Temple (Sakai, Osaka)

255. Stepping-stones, Katsura Imperial Villa

256. Stepping-stones in the garden of Daichiji Temple (Shiga)

257. Paving stones, Saiōin (Kyoto)

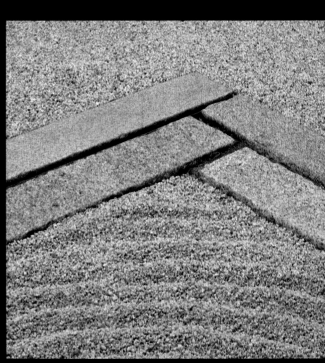

258. Paving stones, Shinnyoin (Kyoto)

259. Bridge of stepping-stones, Heian Jingū Shrine (Kyoto)

260. Stepping-stones, Konjiin, Nanzenji Temple (Kyoto)

261. Stepping-stones, Fushin'an, Omotesenke (Kyoto)

262. Stepping-stones, Katsura Imperial Villa

263. Stone steps

264. Stone steps, Magoji Temple (Wakasa, Fukui)

265. Stone steps, Jingoji Temple (Kyoto)

WASHBASINS

手水鉢

Stone basins stand in the middle of tea gardens. They are called *tsukubai*, which is derived from the verb "to crouch." Guests at a tea ceremony must bow low to wash their hands as part of the ritual of purification.

266. The water basin called Yohobutsu, Urasenke Konnichian, Kyoto.

267. *Chōzu-bachi* in the shape of jujube, Tōkaian (Kyoto)

268. *Chōzu-bachi*, Shōjūraigōji Temple (Shiga)

269. *Chōzu-bachi* in the shape of Buddha's hand, Anyōin (Hyōgo)

270. A water basin in the shape of a *masu* (measure), Katsurarikyu (Kyoto)

271. Ryōnanji-style *chōzu-bachi*, Ryōnanji Temple (Kyoto)

272. *Chōzu-bachi*, Shōiken, Katsura Imperial Villa

273. *Chōzu-bachi*, Saiōin (Kyoto)

274. Water basin called *Ginkakuji-gata* (Ginkakuji original type), Jishoji (Kyoto)

275. *Chōzu-bachi* in the shape of the shell, Kashūji Temple (Kyoto)

276. *Chōzu-bachi*, Kikugetsutei, Kikurinji Temple (Kagawa)

277. *Chōzu-bachi* in the shape of the Chinese character "one," Tōkaian (Kyoto)

278. Fusen-style *chōzu-bachi*, Kohōan (Kyoto)

279. *Chōzu-bachi*, Saiendō Hall, Hōryūji Temple (Nara)

280. *Chōzu-bachi*, Ōyamazumi Shrine (Ehime)

GARDEN LANTERNS

灯籠

Garden lanterns were originally used to illuminate the grounds of Buddhist temples. When the tea ceremony became popular, the lanterns were placed along the path leading to an evening tea gathering.

281. Hanging lantern, Kasuga Grand Shrine (Nara)

282. *Suhama*-style lantern (tōrō) in the garden of the Katsura Imperial Villa

283. *Sankō*-style lantern, Katsura Imperial Villa

284. *Rikyū*-style lantern, Nanshūji Temple (Sakai, Osaka)

285. Triangular lantern, Katsura Imperial Villa

286. *Oribe*-style lantern,
Kuhonji Temple (Kyoto)

287. *Yukumi*-style lantern, the Mori residence (Yamaguchi)

288. *Kotoji* (*yukumi*-style) lantern, Kenrokuen Park (Kanazawa, Ishikawa)

289. Stone lantern, Kondō Hall, Daigoji Temple (Kyoto)

290.
Byōdōin-style lantern (Uji, Kyoto)

291. Stone lantern, Myōkian (Kyoto)

292. Hanging lantern, Heian Jingū Shrine (Kyoto)

293. Hanging lantern, Tanba Kotōkan (Sasayama, Tanba, Kyoto)

294. Hanging lantern, Tōrindo (Osaka)

WALLS AND FENCES

塀・垣

The earlier times, fences and walls did not shut out the world, but were used simply as a divider between house and road. Now, a house surrounded by a bamboo fence or hedge seems peaceful and intimate.

295. *Ginkakuji* fence, Jishoji (or Ginkakuji) Temple

296. Stockade fence, Kohōan (Kyoto)

297. *Teppō* fence, Kiyozumi Teien Garden (Tokyo)

298. *Ōtsu* fence, Kasuikan (Fukushima)

130

299. Brushwood fence, Kairakuen Park (Mito, Ibaraki)

300. *Katsura* fence, Sankeien Park (Yokohama)

301. *Kenninji* fence, Meimeian (Kyoto)

302. The stone wall of a Samurai's residence, Chiran, Kagoshima.

303. Stone wall of the Honma residence (Yamagata)

304. Wall, Myōjōji Temple (Hakui, Ishikawa)

305. Wall, Eihoji Temple (Gifu)

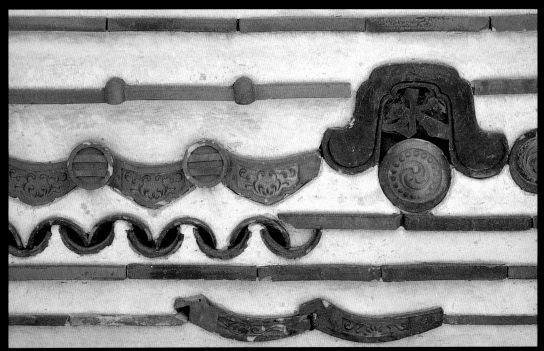

306. Wall, Daitokuji Temple (Kyoto)

307. Wall, Kairyūōji Temple (Nara)

A sacred straw rope (*shimenawa*) is spread so that no impurity will enter a holy place. At New Year, gates become places of dignified beauty when they are hung with new ropes.

308. *Shimenawa* (a sacred Shinto straw festoon), Ōyamazumijinja, Ehime

309. *Shimekazari* (straw festoon) at a private residence (Furuichi, Mie)

310. *Shimenawa* and *shide* (sacred paper) (Tsuruoka, Yamagata)

311. *Shimenawa* and *sakabayashi* (round ball of cedar leaves) at a merchant's house (Narai, Kiso, Nagano)

312. *Kazarinoshi* (paper ornament used as a token of congratulations), Jōnangū Shrine (Kyoto)

313. *Kanjōnawa* (straw festoon to welcome spirits) (Asuka, Nara)

314. *Kanjōnawa*, Enjōji Temple (Nara)

315. *Shimenawa*, Wakasahiko Shrine (Wakasa, Fukui)

316. *Kadomatsu* (pine-and-bamboo New Year's decoration) (Shimabara, Kyoto)

317. *Sakaki*, Ise Jingū Shrine (Mie)

318. *Kamifuda*, Jōnangū Shrine (Kyoto)

319. *Ema* (votive pictures), Futaiji Temple (Nara)

320. *Senja fuda* (visiting cards) on a gate of Chionji Temple (Kyoto)

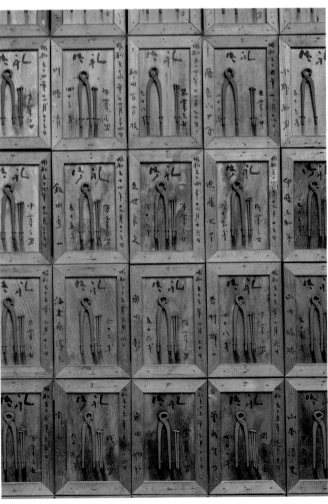

321. *Ema* with eight-inch nails

322. *Omikuji* (written oracles), Shirayamahime Shrine (Tsuruki, Ishikawa)

323. *Omikuji*, Kannonshōji Temple (Shiga)

324. *Senbazuru* (chains of paper cranes), Heiwa Koen (Peace Park) (Hiroshima)

Glossary

amigasamon: one of the gates in a tea-ceremony garden, so named because of its resemblance to the ancient *amigasa*, a kind of bamboo hat

andon: an oil lamp with a paper shade attached to a cube-shaped, cylindrical, or spherical frame. There are *andon* made to be placed on a flat surface, hung from a pillar, or carried.

azekura: a high-floored storehouse whose walls are usually made of triangularly shaped logs placed across one another. Examples still standing are the treasure house of *Shoso-in* Temple, the treasure house and sutra storehouse of *Toshodaiji* Temple, and the treasure house of *Toji* Temple (*Kyoto Gokokuji*).

benigara kabe: a wall painted with *benigara*, or *bengara*, a red cosmetic made by firing yellow clay containing ferric oxide, or rust. The name seems to be derived from Bengal, the region of India where the substance originated.

chōchin: a lamp, often carried, with a paper shade attached to a frame of fine bamboo, inside of which is placed a candle. The frames of early *chōchin* were fixed, but later *chōchin* could be folded.

chōzu-bachi: any of numerous styles of stone basins in a temple, shrine, or garden, containing water (*chōzu*) for washing the face and hands and rinsing the mouth

chūmon: in Buddhist temples, a gate between the main (south) gate and the main part of the temple; in *shinden-zukuri* (Heian residential architecture), a gate between the hallway running from the east wing to the west wing and the hallway to the south wing; in a tea ceremony garden, the gate between the inner and outer gardens

ema: a votive picture tablet. The original custom was to donate a horse to a temple or shrine when making a request; later, a picture (*e*) of a horse (*ma*) was given. Still later, pictures of other things were offered.

funa-dansu: any of several types of chests or cabinets used by seventeenth- to early-twentieth-century captains of transport ships. Specific kinds include the *kakesuzuri*, a small chest for holding money and important papers; the *chōhako*, a small box for storing ledgers and business documents; and the *hanbitsu*, a clothes chest.

fusuma: a sliding door made of a wooden frame faced with paper or cloth. Originally called *fusuma shōji*, as opposed to *akari shōji* (now usually called *shōji*).

gyōki-buki: one form of a tiled roof, possibly named after the Nara period (710–784) monk Gyōki. Concave tiles, one edge of which is thicker than the other, are arranged so that the thin edge of one overlaps the thick edge of the next.

hifumi-ishi: a pattern of pebbles as found on the grounds of the tea-ceremony house at Kyoto Shugakuin Detached Palace

hikite: a cord or metal handle on a sliding door for grasping with the hand

iraka: the highest roof ridge on a house; a roof tile; a tiled roof

irori: a hearth set in the floor

ishi-datami: square or rectangular flagstones set closely together; a place paved with these

kabe: the inner or outer walls of a house, made of earth or wood

kabuto-zukuri: a style of roof thatching on private houses in which the eaves are cut in such a way as to resemble a helmet (*kabuto*)

kaerumata: (lit., frog's crotch): a support resting between two beams, made up of two components: a block on the top resting on a downwardly curved brace reminiscent of a frog's spread legs

kaga noren: a *noren* used in the Kaga region (Ishikawa Prefecture) to separate the main room in the front of a shop from the inner part of the shop. In this region, a bride would bring such a *noren* to her husband's home; after the wedding ceremony, it would be put up in the couple's room. Kaga *noren* were usually made of silk or crepe and were dyed very beautifully, with the bride's family crest. They were also called *hanayome noren* (bride's *noren*).

kaki: a general term for a wall or fence of earth, stone, bamboo, or wood, used to separate one's property from the neighbor's, the road, etc.

kanban: a sign showing a store's name, business, and products. There are various kinds: hanging signs (*sage kanban* or *kake kanban*), roof signs (*yane kanban*), signs placed on the street (*oki kanban*).

karamon: a gateway whose roof is of the *karahafu* style. A *hafu* is an ornament attached to the gable of a roof; a *kara-hafu* is such an ornament in the shape of a somewhat flattened archery bow.

katō mado: a window the top of whose frame is arch shaped, the bottom bell shaped; also called a *Genji mado*. A shape employed in Zen architecture, it was used for temples, castles, and tea-ceremony houses.

katsuogi: a log placed on the ridge or the roof of a Shinto shrine or a palace; with the *chigi* (projecting rafter ends of a shrine's roof), the symbol of a shrine

kawara: a fired piece of clay used as a roof or floor tile.

kayabuki: the process of thatching a roof; a thatched roof

kōshi: latticework of wood or bamboo arranged crosswise, used for doors and windows

kōshi-do: a door with latticework

machiai: a building belonging to a tea-ceremony house where guests wait. If in the outer garden, it is called a *hakamatsuke*, *yoritsuke*, or *soto machiai*; if in the inner garden, a *koshikake*, *koshikake machiai*, *uchi machiai*, or *chūritsu machiai*.

maira-do: in *shoin-zukuri*, a sliding door made of a thin board to which is attached, either vertically or horizontally, thin strips of wood closely spaced.

mizuya: a chest of drawers for tea things and tableware

mune: the ridge of a roof

munekazari: a decoration placed on the ridge of a roof

nagamochi: a long trunk for storing clothes and supplies; carried on poles by two people

nakakuguri: a gate in the garden of a tea-ceremony house, between the inner and outer gardens; one kind of *chūmon*. Guests must stoop to pass through it.

namako kabe: a style of wall used for storehouses and the like in which square tiles are attached to the wall with *shikkui*, the *shikkui* being allowed to protrude in a semi-conical shape from the space between the tiles.

noren: a curtain hung in front of a shop as protection from sunlight and wind, and to afford some privacy. It was perhaps originally used by Zen temples as protection from wind and cold. Beginning in the Edo period (1603–1867), business establishments designed their own *noren* with words, figures, and pictures dyed in the fabric.

onigawara (lit., ogre tile): a clay gargoyle, usually in the shape of an ogre's face. Old ones had lotus or animal figures carved in them.

orido: a folding door

ōtemon: the main gate of a castle

ranma: latticework or a board with a figure carved through it placed between the ceiling and the lintel or *nageshi* to let in light and air, or used as a decoration

renji mado: a style of window to which is attached *renji*, a form of latticework that uses bamboo or wood arranged either vertically or horizontally. Renji mado were used originally in Zen architecture, then for tea-ceremony houses.

rojimon: the gate at the entrance to a tea-ceremony garden

sakabayashi: bundled Japanese cedar (*sugi*) leaves hung from the edge of the eaves of a saké brewer's shop, used as a sort of *kanban*

senja fuda: tags of paper attached to shrine doors and pillars by pilgrims making the rounds of many shrines. The pilgrim's name, address, and business are printed on the tags by the wood-block process.

shachihoko: a clay or metal ornament in the shape of a legendary fish with its tail curved up, placed at the end of the ridge of a roof. Its head is that of a dragon or tiger; on its back are sharp spines.

shide: paper hung from branches or *shimenawa*. Originally paper made from the bark of the paper mulberry tree (*kōzo*) was used for *shide*; now ordinary paper is.

shiki-ishi: a flat stone used for paving; a flagstone

shikkui: a plaster-like substance made of a mixture of lime, clay, and plant fibers to which funori (a glue made from seaweeds) is added; used to attach bricks, etc., to walls, floors, and ceilings

shimenawa: a straw rope hung at a shrine or Shinto ceremony to prevent impurity from entering the area. The rope is usually twisted counterclockwise; at regular intervals the ends of the straw are pulled out and allowed to hang down; between these, sacred paper (*shide*) is hung.

shitomi-do: a latticed door hanging down from a *nageshi*, swung up and down, either toward the inside or the outside. Also called simply *shitomi*. *Nageshi* is a long horizontal piece of wood on the upper part of a wall, connecting two pillars, originally used as the support for a *shitomi-do*, but now for decorative purposes.

shoin: in early China, a place for reading and research; in Japan, a part of a temple used for reading and giving lectures; during and after the Muromachi period (1336–1573), the study in a warrior or noble's home

shoin-zukuri: a form of Japanese residential architecture developed from the end of the Muromachi period to the Momoyama period (1579–1600). Based on the *shoin* of Zen temples, it was used for the homes of warriors and nobles. In the style, one house is made up of several rooms; the main room has a floor, shelves, and *shoin-doko* (a small, protruding room off the main room, with *shoji* windows). Tatami are placed snugly into the floor, and square framing is used for the *shōji* and *fusuma*.

shoji: a general term for any partition, such as a *fusuma* and a *tsuitate* (free-standing wooden screen). The word is now used mostly to signify *akari shōji*, sliding doors on whose frames are pasted translucent paper to allow light to pass through.

shokudai: a candlestand

sōrin: the set of metal ornaments on the spire of a pagoda. Supported by the pagoda's main pillar, the *sorin*'s components, from base to top, are the *fukuhachi*, the *ukebana*, nine rings (*kurin*), the *suien*, the *ryūsha*, and the *hōshu*. Also called *kurin*.

sugido: a sliding door made of a single board, often Japanese cedar (*sugi*)

tebunko: a small box for holding letters and writing materials

tenshukaku: the keep, or *donjon*, of a castle; a high tower located in the center or a corner of the inner citadel. During war, it was used as an observatory or as the last defense holdout; during peace, as a daimyo's residence and symbol of authority.

teppō hazama: a hole in the wall through which a gun can be shot; a gunport

teshoku: a candlestand with a long handle

tobi-ishi: stepping stones; either natural or cut

tokonoma: an alcove, raised slightly above floor level, in which a scroll might be hung or a vase placed

tokyō: a wooden frame placed on the top of a pillar to support the eaves of a building, comprised of a square or rectangular support and a horizontal bracket

torii: a gateway at the entrance to a Shinto shrine symbolizing that the grounds are holy. There is a pillar on either side and two crossbeams at the top, the upper beam called the *kasagi*, the lower beam the *nuki*.

tōrō: a lantern. Originally for illuminating a temple priest's living quarters, *tōrō* later came to be used to light and decorate temples, shrines, and gardens. They are made of iron, copper, ceramic, stone, bamboo, and wood; there are *tōrō* for hanging and for setting on a surface; they come in various shapes.